Specific Skill Series
for Language Arts

Paragraphs

Leveled Books
in Nine Key
Language Arts Skill Areas

Columbus, OH

The **McGraw·Hill** Companies

SRAonline.com

 SRA

Send all inquiries to:
SRA/McGraw-Hill
8787 Orion Place
Columbus, OH 43240-4027

Printed in the United States of America.

ISBN 0-07-601671-4

2 3 4 5 6 7 8 9 MAZ 08 07 06 05

GENERAL INFORMATION ON PARAGRAPHS

Writers need to understand and apply the rules governing paragraphs in order to write effectively. A piece of writing with correct paragraphing helps the reader by breaking up long sections of prose and arranging ideas into more easily comprehended units. Writing strong paragraphs involves knowing that most paragraphs require a topic sentence and supporting sentences and that different types of paragraphs, such as narrative, descriptive, expository, and persuasive, have different purposes.

Common problems students have when writing paragraphs include the following:

- **Too short:** Paragraphs that contain only one to three normal sentences seem choppy and interruptive to the reader.
- **Too long:** Students who write overly long paragraphs might not understand the conventional structure of paragraphs.
- **Incoherence:** These paragraphs skip from idea to idea with no logical framework.

ABOUT *SPECIFIC SKILL SERIES FOR LANGUAGE ARTS*

Specific Skill Series for Language Arts is a companion to *Specific Skill Series,* a supplemental reading program that has been widely recognized for its effectiveness for over thirty years. The two series are designed and organized the same. *Specific Skill Series for Language Arts* consists of discrete units of practice exercises that target and reinforce fundamental language-arts skills. Units in both series are presented in multiple-choice format for standardized test practice.

ABOUT *PARAGRAPHS*

The scope and sequence for Books A through H of *Paragraphs* focuses on the purposes, planning, and structure of paragraphs. The scope and sequence for each book is located on the last page of the book. Each unit includes

- **rule boxes** that explain skills related to writing paragraphs.
- **models** in each rule box to illustrate the skills being discussed.
- **multiple-choice exercises** for skills practice and reinforcement.

Four **Language Activity Pages** (LAPs) appear in each book. Each LAP is divided into the following four sections and reviews the skills practiced in the preceding units:

Exercising Your Skill reviews key terms and concepts.

Expanding Your Skill provides mixed practice.

Exploring Language shows how the skills apply to real-world contexts by featuring one of six forms of writing: descriptive, narrative, personal, persuasive, expository, and poetry.

Expressing Yourself includes two creative activities related to the skills. One activity is always a Work-with-a-Partner activity to encourage collaborative learning.

SERIES COMPONENTS

- **Student Editions:** Nine books in each level (A–H) focus on nine skill areas: *Grammar, Usage, Mechanics, Spelling, Vocabulary, Sentences, Paragraphs, Writing Process,* and *Research.*

- **Placement Test Books:** One book for each skill area includes diagnostic tests to place students in the correct level.

- **Teacher's Manual:** Primarily an answer key, the *Teacher's Manual* also includes reproducible student worksheets and further information on how to use the program, including classroom management tips.

HOW TO USE *SPECIFIC SKILL SERIES FOR LANGUAGE ARTS*

Placing Students in Levels: The scope and sequence, complexity of skills, and readability in Levels A through H correspond to Grades 1 through 8. Students may, however, be placed in <u>any level</u>. For example, in the second grade, a student who needs remedial work in a specific skill may be placed in Book A, an on-level student who would benefit from skills reinforcement may be placed in Book B, and an advanced student who is ready for enrichment may be placed in Book C or higher. *Placement Tests* help place students in the correct level.

Setting: This series can be used for independent study and one-on-one practice sessions, as well as in small-group and whole-class settings. It is also effective in after-school and summer-school programs.

Getting Started: Students must have notebook paper or copies of reproducible student worksheets (located in the *Teacher's Manual*) before they begin working. Remind students not to write in the books. Students may begin in any unit of any book, depending on the skill practice they need, although it is recommended that they begin with Unit 1. As they work through the units, students should record their answers on notebook paper or on the student worksheets.

Pacing: Students should be encouraged to work at their own pace, completing a few units every day or every other day.

Scoring: Teachers should score units as soon as they have been completed. Then a discussion can be held in which students justify their answer choices.

Internet Use: Some activities, especially those in *Research,* require students to use the Internet. Students' use of the Internet should be monitored closely for content appropriateness and safety.

This book will show you how to write a paragraph. A paragraph is a group of sentences about the same topic. Most paragraphs have a beginning, a middle, and an end.

BEGINNING

I like grasshoppers. They are a nice green or brown color. They eat only leaves. They are small, but they can jump high. Did you know that they can also sing? I think grasshoppers are great.

MIDDLE

END

In Book A *Paragraphs,* you will learn about
- Types of Paragraphs
- Using a Web
- Topic Sentences
- Details
- Closing Sentences
- Complete Paragraphs
- Staying on Topic
- Time and Order Words

After you finish this book, you will be able to write paragraphs that describe, convince, give facts, explain how to do something, or tell part of a story.

A **paragraph** is a group of sentences about the same topic. A paragraph's purpose can be
- to describe something.
- to share facts or ideas that are true.
- to explain or tell how to do something.

Read each paragraph. What is its purpose?

1. A square has four sides. A triangle has three sides. Each side of a square is the same length. The sides of a triangle can be different lengths.
   (A) to tell how to do something
   (B) to share facts

2. Tigers are very large cats. They have sharp teeth and claws. Tigers are very strong. They have light fur with dark stripes.
   (A) to describe
   (B) to tell how to do something

3.　You should plan a poster before you make it. Use a pencil to write words and draw pictures. You can erase what you do not like. Use crayons to trace what you do like.

(A) to share facts

(B) to tell how to do something

4.　My address is 171 Elm Street. This is how to get to my house from school. First walk two blocks past the park. Then turn left on Elm Street. My house is white and green.

(A) to describe

(B) to tell how to do something

5.　My favorite shirt is blue. It has one pocket on the front. It has five buttons. My favorite shirt has short sleeves. It is very soft.

(A) to describe

(B) to tell how to do something

Read each paragraph. What is its purpose?

6.   The beach is my favorite place. I like to feel the warm, soft sand. I love to hear the waves splash. I watch the birds and feel the sun on my face.

(A) to tell how to do something

(B) to share ideas that are true

7.   Zebras are the size of small horses. They have tails and short manes. Zebras are white with black or brown stripes.

(A) to tell how to do something

(B) to describe

8.   I brush my teeth a few times each day. It keeps them clean. I floss my teeth too. Brushing and flossing keep my teeth strong.

(A) to share facts

(B) to tell how to do something

9.   Turn on the oven. Put the dough in a pan. Wear an oven mitt to put the pan in the oven. Bake the bread for twenty minutes.

(A) to tell how to do something

(B) to describe

10.   Oak toads live in forests. You can usually see them during the day. Oak toads are very small. They make a noise like a baby bird.

(A) to tell how to do something

(B) to share facts

11.   Winter can be cold. It can snow. The wind is chilly. Winter is a good time for warm soup.

(A) to share ideas that are true

(B) to tell how to do something

12.   Blue whales are the largest animals on Earth. They live in seas and oceans. Even though they are big, whales swim well.

(A) to share facts

(B) to tell how to do something

More purposes for writing a paragraph are
- to tell a make-believe or a true story.
- to convince, or make you think a certain way.

A paragraph's sentences are on the same topic.

Read each paragraph. What is its purpose?

1.   Swimming can be fun. It is also good exercise. It is not safe to be near water if you cannot swim. There are classes that teach swimming. It is a good idea to learn how to swim.

   (A) to make you think a certain way

   (B) to tell a make-believe story

2.   A fox the size of a mouse sat under a tree. He looked up and saw apples. The fox jumped as high as he could, but he did not get an apple.

   (A) to convince

   (B) to tell a make-believe story

3.   Our cat had kittens. Two kittens are black, and one has spots. Each kitten is tiny and soft.

(A) to tell a true story

(B) to convince

4.   Ben and Nick camped in Ben's backyard one night. They heard a noise by the tent. Ben got a flashlight. They saw a rabbit and laughed.

(A) to make you think a certain way

(B) to tell a true story

5.   Fruits and vegetables are good for you. You can put fruit on cereal. You can put vegetables on salads. Eat fruits and vegetables every day!

(A) to tell a make-believe story

(B) to convince

6.   One day, it rained grape jelly! I ran inside to get my umbrella. The jelly stuck to everything. I hope it does not rain peanut butter tomorrow!

(A) to tell a make-believe story

(B) to make you think a certain way

Read each paragraph. What is its purpose?

7. Reading is fun! You can pretend to be other people when you read. You can visit new places. You can learn a lot too. I think it is a great idea to read as much as you can.
(A) to convince
(B) to tell a true story

8. I keep my room neat. I put away my toys and clothes. Then I always know where to find them. I have more room to play when things are put back. It helps to keep rooms neat.
(A) to convince
(B) to tell a make-believe story

9. My cat Buster was asleep by a window inside our house. We were playing catch outside. A ball hit near the window. Buster jumped and hid under my bed.
(A) to tell a make-believe story
(B) to tell a true story

10.　　Dogs make great pets. They are happy to see their owners. They like to run and play. A dog can be your best pal.

(A) to make you think a certain way

(B) to tell a make-believe story

11.　　Yesterday there was a camel in the store where I work. His name was Harold. He did not buy anything, but he asked where the closest library was. He wanted to read a book.

(A) to tell a true story

(B) to tell a make-believe story

12.　　I was walking my dog in the park one day. The sky grew dark very quickly. Rain poured down and I heard thunder. My dog and I ran and found shelter.

(A) to make you think a certain way

(B) to tell a true story

A **web** helps to plan ideas for a paragraph. The **topic,** or main idea, of a paragraph is written in the middle circle of a web. **Details,** or ideas about the topic, are written in the other circles. In a web, details can be words or sentences.

Read each web. Choose the missing idea.

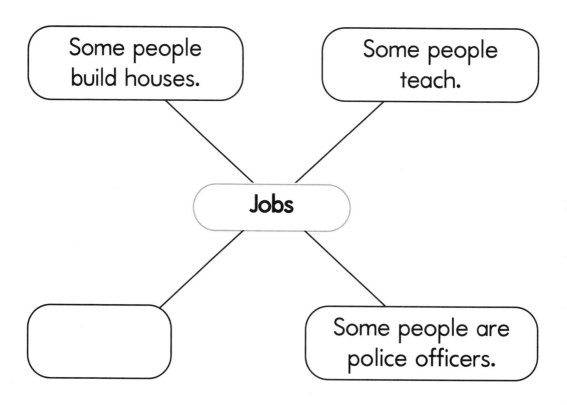

Some people build houses.

Some people teach.

Jobs

Some people are police officers.

1. **(A)** Some people fight fires.
   (B) I like to read.
   (C) The museum can be fun.

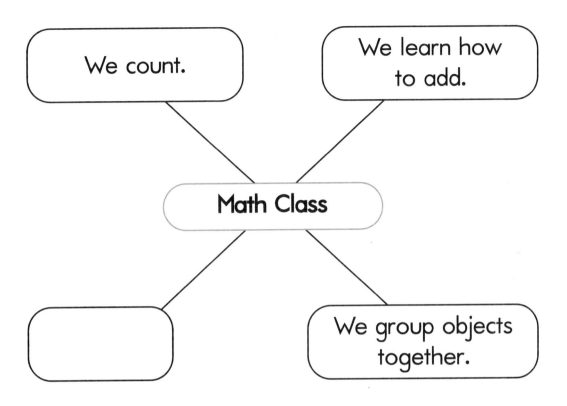

We count.

We learn how to add.

Math Class

We group objects together.

2. **(A)** We learn how to paint.

(B) I study science after spelling.

(C) We learn how to subtract.

Read each web. Choose the missing idea.

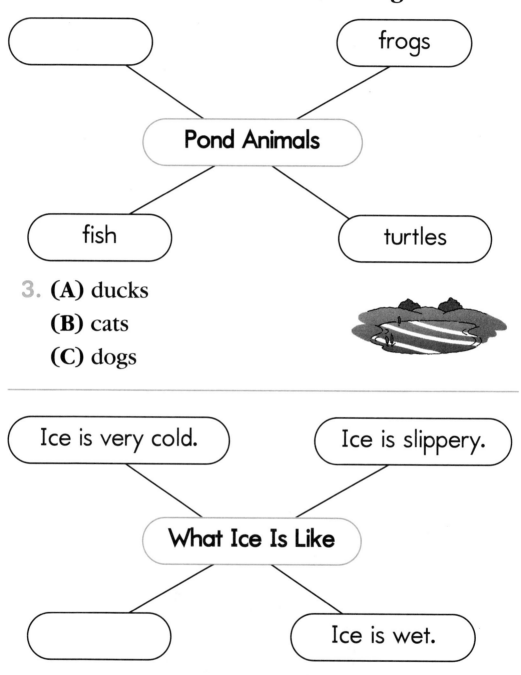

frogs

Pond Animals

fish

turtles

3. **(A)** ducks
   (B) cats
   (C) dogs

Ice is very cold.

Ice is slippery.

What Ice Is Like

Ice is wet.

4. **(A)** Snow is light.
   (B) Ice can be clear.
   (C) You do not skate on snow.

16

Read each web. Which idea does *not* belong?

5.

(**A**) There were penguins.

(**B**) We ate lunch by the swans.

Our Trip to the Zoo

(**C**) We saw elephants.

(**D**) My homework is in a folder.

6.

(**A**) The sun is in the sky.

(**B**) We see the moon.

What We See in the Sky

(**C**) It is fun to visit the playground.

(**D**) Sometimes there are rainbows.

Read each web. Which idea does *not* belong?

7.
(A) Many people watch basketball.

(B) Each team has nine players on the field.

Rules of Baseball

(C) A batter is out after three strikes.

(D) There are three bases and home plate.

8.
(A) apples

(B) oranges

Fruits That Grow on Trees

(C) peas

(D) bananas

9.

(A) eating fruits and vegetables

(B) the library and post office

Things That Are Good for the Body

(C) exercising and drinking water

(D) getting enough sleep

10.

(A) Some people have dogs.

(B) Some people have fish.

Kinds of Pets

(C) Some people have cats.

(D) Some people ride bikes.

A. Exercising Your Skill

Number your paper from 1 to 4. Read each sentence below. Use a word from the box only once to fill in each blank correctly.

Webs	paragraph	true	topic

1. A ___ is a group of sentences about the same topic.

2. A paragraph can tell a ___ or a make-believe story.

3. ___ help to plan ideas for paragraphs.

4. A paragraph's ___ is also its main idea.

B. Expanding Your Skill

Read the web below. What is its topic? On your paper, write the two ideas that do *not* belong.

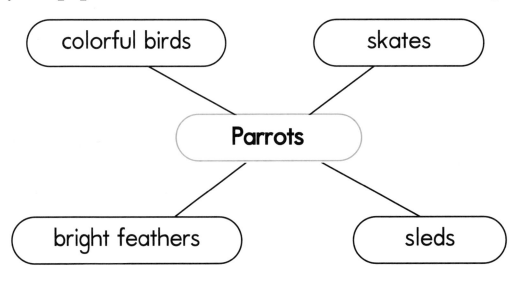

C. Exploring Language

Expository Writing Read the paragraph below. Write the three sentences that are *not* about its topic.

A Pet Parrot

To care for a parrot, change the paper on the bottom of its cage each day. I play with toys. Parrots should have fresh food and water. I eat fruit. Spend time with the parrot. I lost a watch. Let a parrot out of its cage only if someone is with it.

D. Expressing Yourself

Do one of these things. When you are done, give your paper to your teacher.

1. If a web's topic is *Cats,* one of its details could be *Cats purr.* Write three other details that would belong on a web about cats.

2. [WORK with a PARTNER] Find a partner. Look at the web in Part B. Draw your own web with a middle circle and four other circles. Write the topic *Dogs* where it belongs on the web. Then write a detail in each of the web's other circles.

A **topic sentence** tells the main idea of a paragraph or what the paragraph is about. It is usually the first sentence of a paragraph.

Topic: My Art Teacher

Topic Sentence: Mr. Boyd is my art teacher.

Which topic sentence belongs at the beginning of each paragraph?

1.   We went on a boat ride. We saw dolphins flip through the air! Once back on land, we had a picnic. I hope we go again!

(A) Our family had a nice vacation.

(B) Our family saw a movie.

(C) Our family cooked dinner.

2.   I love to see snow on the ground and on trees. I do not mind cold weather. I like to go sledding. I also like to build with snow.

(A) Summer is very hot.

(B) Winter is my favorite season.

(C) I do not like winter.

3.   Look at the sky, toward the rain. The sun should be behind you. You might see different colors that curve across the sky.

(A) You see clouds when it rains.

(B) A rainbow can be in the sky when it rains.

(C) It never rains in the summer.

4.   Following rules helps keep us safe. Rules can help us get along with others.

(A) The game is fun.

(B) Police officers do not make rules.

(C) It is good to have rules.

5.   We drove to a campground. My mom put up our tent. My brother and I got our grill from the van. We all helped Dad fix dinner.

(A) My family went camping last summer.

(B) Hiking is fun.

(C) Tennis is my favorite sport.

Which topic sentence belongs at the beginning of each paragraph?

6.   I wake up and get out of bed. I pick out my clothes and get dressed. I eat breakfast. I wash my face and brush my teeth. I make my lunch. I put my lunch and homework in my backpack. I check to see if I need an umbrella.

(A) Here is how I get ready for school.

(B) I like making lunch better than buying it.

(C) I do my homework before I play.

7.   Henry plays the flute. Kayla plays the guitar. Mitch plays the drums. Each person takes turns singing. Sometimes the band practices after school.

(A) I love to listen to music.

(B) I am learning to play the piano.

(C) There are three people in the band.

8.   Ships are large boats. Canoes are small boats. Speedboats can be many sizes.

(A) There are many types of boats.

(B) Oceans are filled with saltwater.

(C) You can paddle a canoe.

9.   Sometimes we make a fort with blocks. Sometimes we make a fort with pillows. We make snow forts in winter too.

(A) Blocks can be many shapes.

(B) My sister and I like to play in the snow.

(C) My sister and I like to build forts.

10.   Some apples are red. Some grapes are purple. Most bananas are yellow.

(A) I love bananas!

(B) Fruits can be different colors.

(C) You should eat some fruit every day.

Unit 5
Topic Sentences

A topic sentence tells a paragraph's main idea.

Which topic sentence belongs at the beginning of each paragraph?

1.   Sometimes I fly a kite. If the ducks are in the pond, I watch them. I also like to sit on a swing at the park.

    (A) The park is far from my house.
    (B) There are many things to do at the park.
    (C) It is not hard to make a kite.

2.   They slip and slide on the ice. They dive into the water. They are good swimmers.
    (A) There are many kinds of pools.
    (B) Penguins can lay eggs.
    (C) Penguins are playful animals.

3.   It is warm from the oven. It smells very good. The muffin will taste yummy!
    (A) The blueberry muffin is fresh.
    (B) Here is how to make a muffin.
    (C) We do not like muffins.

4.   Crystal likes to go fast. Bonnie does not mind going slow. Their horses like to run.

(A) The trail is long.

(B) Horses have pretty tails.

(C) The sisters like to ride horses.

5.   She gathered wheat. She made the wheat into flour. The hen used the flour to make dough. Then she baked bread.

(A) Once there was a hen that baked bread.

(B) Once there was a hen that liked wheat.

(C) Once there was a hen that had five chicks.

6.   I put on my raincoat and hat. I put on my boots and get my umbrella. I am ready to go outside.

(A) This is how I get ready for the beach.

(B) This is how I get ready to be in the rain.

(C) Rain can be good for plants.

Which topic sentence belongs at the beginning of each paragraph?

7.   Sometimes they use circle and square patterns. They can add triangles and stars too.

(A) Cole and Kristi make patterns with shapes.

(B) Their favorite subject is math.

(C) Cole and Kristi like to read poems.

8.   Lobsters and shrimp live in the ocean. Sharks and whales live there. Crabs and clams live in the ocean too.

(A) There are no living things in the ocean.

(B) Only fish live in the ocean.

(C) The ocean is full of living things.

9.   Tree leaves begin to grow. Grass turns from brown to green. Other plants rise from the ground in spring.

(A) Brown is the color of spring.

(B) Many things change in spring.

(C) Baby animals are born in spring.

10. My grandparents are coming over for dinner. My aunt and uncle are coming too. Some cousins will be at dinner.

(A) We are having a family dinner.

(B) We are going to the zoo.

(C) My grandparents live in Colorado.

11. I look at lots of new books. I read quietly in the library. I can check out books to take home.

(A) I like to go to the store.

(B) I like to buy shoes.

(C) I like to go to the library.

12. I brush my teeth. I take a bath. I put on my pajamas. I say good night to my family. I turn off the light and get into bed.

(A) This is what I do before I go to sleep.

(B) This is what I do when I wake up.

(C) This is what I do when I eat lunch.

In a paragraph, **details** are sentences that give information about the topic.

Topic Sentence: I have a new poetry book.

Detail: The book's poetry is about nature.

Read each topic sentence. Choose its detail.

1. Melinda has a pet dog.

    (A) I put a clean dish on the table.

    (B) Her dog is brown with white spots.

    (C) Manny and his cat play with a toy.

2. The new ice rink is open.

    (A) The newspaper is on the porch.

    (B) It looks like it might rain today.

    (C) Penny and Frank went there to ice-skate.

3. My dad has a very old wagon.

    (A) The wheels on the wagon squeak.

    (B) Bicycles have pedals.

    (C) The tree in the front yard is tall.

4. Aunt Marie and Uncle Barney live in Ohio.

    (A) I have never been on a train.

    (B) Illinois is west of Ohio.

    (C) We camp with them in Ohio twice a year.

5. Many frogs live by our pond.

    (A) My sister cut the grass.

    (B) We see frogs that are as big as apples!

    (C) I took out the trash.

6. I will be in second grade next year.

    (A) My teacher will be Miss Roth.

    (B) I bought my lunch yesterday.

    (C) My mother is a dentist.

7. We make breakfast together on weekends.

    (A) She finished her homework.

    (B) His book is in the car.

    (C) Our kitchen usually smells like waffles.

Read each topic sentence. Choose its detail.

8. Our neighbor Oliver has a vegetable garden.

   (A) He gives his extra green peppers to us.

   (B) The bird flew away quickly.

   (C) She does not think it will snow.

9. The flowers in the park bloomed.

   (A) Their petals are white and purple.

   (B) Winter is a nice time of year.

   (C) Sometimes rain smells good.

10. A new movie theater opened in town.

   (A) That road is closed until Friday.

   (B) The team has a surprise for the coach.

   (C) The seats in the theater are cozy.

11. I saw a yellow chick.

   (A) These pants are too short.

   (B) The chick looked fluffy and soft.

   (C) Her family had a yard sale.

12. The market had fresh apples.

    (A) It is too warm inside the truck.

    (B) The bank is near his home.

    (C) One of the apples tasted sour.

13. There is a new boss at work.

    (A) I listen to music as I clean my room.

    (B) We hung a sign to greet her.

    (C) There are many spoons in this drawer.

14. We went to pick cherries on Saturday.

    (A) The rock feels heavy.

    (B) The cherries smelled sweet.

    (C) Those papers are wet.

15. The school's picnic is tomorrow.

    (A) There will be snacks, juice, and games!

    (B) My brother and I moved the desk.

    (C) He cannot find the magazine.

Read each paragraph. Choose the detail that does *not* belong.

16. My favorite color is green. **(A)** I like green apples and green beans. **(B)** I like green hats and green socks. **(C)** The door is locked.

17. We looked at the sky last night. **(A)** They brought Marty to my game. **(B)** The stars were bright. **(C)** The moon was not full.

18. Our teacher grows sunflowers. **(A)** She showed a sunflower to us. **(B)** The chair is broken. **(C)** The sunflower was tall and pretty.

19. There are many kinds of nuts. **(A)** Some nuts can taste salty. **(B)** Other nuts can taste sweet. **(C)** I zipped the suitcase.

20. It is nice to knock before you open a door.
(A) You would not want to scare anyone.
(B) The box is here. (C) People may
not be home to open the door.

21. The car needs a new tire. (A) One tire has a
nail stuck in it. (B) He will read this book
again. (C) It is not safe to drive on a bad tire.

22. A valley is a low area of ground. (A) A valley
can be between mountains. (B) A valley can
be between hills. (C) Fish swim well.

23. There are two May birthdays in my family.
(A) I wrote a note. (B) My dad's birthday is
May 13. (C) My brother's birthday is May 27.

24. Sandra plays the piano. (A) You like to play
kickball. (B) She practices many times a week.
(C) My mom is Sandra's piano teacher.

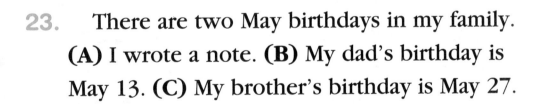

A. Exercising Your Skill

Number your paper from 1 to 3. Read each sentence below. Use a word from the box only once to fill in each blank correctly.

sentence	details	topic

1. A topic ＿＿ tells the main idea of a paragraph or what the paragraph is about.

2. To stay on ＿＿, the rest of the sentences in a paragraph should tell about the main idea.

3. Sentences in the rest of a paragraph are ＿＿.

B. Expanding Your Skill

Write **A, B,** or **C** on your paper to choose the topic sentence for the beginning of this paragraph.

African elephants have larger bodies than Asian, or Indian, elephants. Their ears are larger too. African elephants are gray to brown. Asian elephants are usually dark gray.

(A) Elephants know how to swim.
(B) African and Asian elephants look different.
(C) Elephants are named for where they live.

C. Exploring Language

Expository Writing Number your paper from 1 to 5. Read the paragraph below. Write the letter of the topic sentence. Then write the letter of each detail that does *not* give information about the topic.

(A) Elephants use their trunks for many things. (B) Elephants pick up food with their trunks. (C) Turtles have shells. (D) They use their trunks to get water. (E) Apes are strong. (F) Cheetahs have spots. (G) Elephants use their trunks to touch and talk with each other. (H) Fish live in water.

D. Expressing Yourself

Do one of these things. When you are done, give your paper to your teacher.

1. Draw an elephant. Write a topic sentence and two more details about your drawing.

2. WORK with a PARTNER With a partner, write three words to describe elephants. Then write a topic sentence about elephants. Together, write three details about elephants, using the words you wrote.

A **closing sentence** sums up the main idea of a paragraph or what the writer thinks of the topic. It is usually the last sentence of a paragraph.

Topic: Going to the Park

Closing Sentence: That is why I go to the park.

Which closing sentence belongs at the end of each paragraph?

1. The soccer team practices a lot. They stretch to warm up before they run. They pass the ball on the field. They drink plenty of water.
   (A) The field gets too wet in the rain.
   (B) The basketball team practices inside.
   (C) The soccer team works hard to play well.

2. My mom likes to ski on snow. She makes sure to wear very warm clothes. She wears a hat, gloves, and sunglasses too.
   (A) People can ski on water.
   (B) My mom protects herself from the cold.
   (C) Snow melts if it is too warm outside.

3.   Animal dens can be holes below the ground. They are dug by the animals that use them. Some animals hide and sleep in dens.

(A) Dens help keep animals safe.

(B) Many animals are very strong.

(C) We have a television in our den at home.

4.   Evan packed his bag for gym class. He packed a clean shirt and shorts. He put gym socks and shoes in his bag.

(A) Evan went to the store with his dad.

(B) Evan has a sister named Gloria.

(C) Evan is ready for gym class.

5.   Chris likes to look for birds. She uses a pair of binoculars to see far away. Binoculars can make things look closer than they are.

(A) Our pool will be cleaned tomorrow.

(B) Binoculars can help Chris find birds.

(C) Chris has been in a hot-air balloon.

Which closing sentence belongs at the end of each paragraph?

6.   Our class saw a play yesterday. A lady in the play was sad because her pet was lost. She cried a lot. Luckily there was a happy ending.

(A) My brother is in the third grade.

(B) The lady found her pet.

(C) We have two pages of spelling homework.

7.   If there is a path, it helps to walk on it. This way you do not hurt grass, flowers, or plants. A path is usually less dirty. If you walk on a path, you should not get lost or scare animals.

(A) They worked in the yard on Sunday.

(B) This weather is good for plants.

(C) It is a good idea to walk on paths.

8.   I have a friend named Angelo. He likes to look at leaves. We look at them together. He lives on my street. We ride our bikes.

(A) Angelo and I have fun.

(B) My dad's bike is red.

(C) My bike is blue.

9.   I eat apples. Some apples are crunchy. Other apples are soft. They can be sweet or sour.
(A) They have never made applesauce.
(B) Apples are also good for you.
(C) Oranges grow on trees.

10.   Toys can go in a box. Clothes can go in a closet. Craft supplies can go in a drawer.
(A) The bag is on the chair.
(B) There are many places to put things.
(C) I need a new ruler.

11.   Ted has many books. He reads about bikes. He reads about people. He reads about cats.
(A) Ted likes to read.
(B) His bedroom door is not shut.
(C) Our school has a library.

12.   We have a new car. It has more room in it. My parents bought it for long trips.
(A) Your sister is taking a nap.
(B) The garage windows are dirty.
(C) We will take the car to Arizona next June.

Which closing sentence belongs at the end of each paragraph?

13.   A vet is a special doctor for animals. Phoebe helps the vet. She keeps the dog safe until the vet comes back to the room.

(A) Phoebe would like to be a vet someday.

(B) It is hot outside.

(C) I cannot see the clock.

14.   We get ready for the beach. We take towels and sunscreen. We take snacks and pails.

(A) He is learning how to swim.

(B) The beach is a nice place to spend a day.

(C) The bird landed on that tree branch.

15.   It is time to set the table. Ron has cups. Cal has plates. Dad has knives and spoons.

(A) Tomorrow is your birthday.

(B) Lauren is at the store.

(C) The table needs forks and napkins.

16.   Lyle dreams in his sleep. He dreams of his favorite things. Lyle likes animals.

(A) I have a very soft pillow.

(B) Kate read a poem.

(C) He dreams of lions, monkeys, and whales.

17.   A train is one way to get somewhere. Trains travel on tracks. They go through small towns. They go through big cities.

(A) The bus is big and yellow.

(B) Trains are very helpful.

(C) We flew on an airplane once.

18.   Yogurt is a yummy treat. There are many flavors of yogurt. I like strawberry yogurt. Peach yogurt is good too.

(A) I put cereal in my yogurt for breakfast.

(B) There is juice in the cup.

(C) I like wheat bread with blueberry jam.

A **complete paragraph** should have a topic sentence, details, and a closing sentence.

> I like my math teacher. Her name is Mrs. Zane. She helps us add and subtract. We count blocks too. Mrs. Zane is nice and helpful.

Which sentence completes each paragraph?

1. It was windy today. Mei and Emma went outside. _____ Mei and Emma took their kite to the park. It was a great day to fly a kite!
   (A) They decided to fly a kite.
   (B) They decided to go skating.
   (C) They decided to eat lunch.

2. Bees live and work together. Bees live in hives. Thousands of bees can live in one hive. Some bees work to make honey. _____
   (A) The flowers are blooming.
   (B) I do not like the sound bees make.
   (C) Other bees care for the hive.

3.   Ant gathers food for winter. Ant rests at night. ⎯⎯⎯⎯ Ant sleeps on his bed.

(A) There are different kinds of ants.

(B) Ant goes into his home.

(C) I do not know what ants eat.

4.   Ducks live near lakes and ponds. They use their webbed feet to move in water. ⎯⎯⎯⎯ They get food from the lake or pond.

(A) The sun is shining.

(B) Special feathers keep ducks warm and dry.

(C) Chickens have wings.

5.   Tools can make gardening easier. We use a rake to get leaves. ⎯⎯⎯⎯ We use a hose to water.

(A) We use a shovel to dig.

(B) We sweep the kitchen.

(C) We smell the flowers.

6.   Giraffes are tall animals. They have long legs. Giraffes also have long necks. ⎯⎯⎯⎯

(A) There are many animals in Africa.

(B) Elephants are large.

(C) This way, giraffes can reach tree leaves.

Which sentence completes each paragraph?

7.   Lee and Sara planned a surprise party. It was for their friend Alex's birthday. _____ Then they all shouted, "Happy Birthday!"

(A) Lee likes to draw.

(B) Sara cleaned her room.

(C) The guests hid before Alex got there.

8.   Prince Pierre walked in the woods. He saw a deer and followed it. _____ He stopped to think about how to find his way home.

(A) Pierre has a sister.

(B) Soon Pierre was lost in the woods.

(C) The prince has many horses.

9.   The United States has symbols. The American flag stands for the fifty states. The Liberty Bell stands for freedom. _____

(A) The Statue of Liberty stands for hope.

(B) The White House is a large place.

(C) Green, white, and red are on Mexico's flag.

10.   Milk is good for your health. It helps to build strong bones. _____ It is also used for cooking with other foods. I like milk.

(A) Apple juice tastes sweet.

(B) Water is good for you.

(C) Milk is good for teeth.

11.   Coins are money. A penny is worth one cent. A nickel is worth five cents. _____ A quarter is worth twenty-five cents.

(A) A dime is worth ten cents.

(B) We went shopping.

(C) Paper money can be folded.

12.   There are many ways to get places. You can walk. You can jog or run. You can bike. You can skate. You can drive. _____

(A) My brother's car is black.

(B) You can also fly in an airplane.

(C) I like to sing.

Which sentence completes each paragraph?

13.   It was a stormy night. I was in my room. I heard rain on the roof. _____ Lightning lit up the sky. I hid under my blankets.

(A) The birds were chirping.

(B) I heard loud thunder.

(C) I like soft blankets.

14.   A garage helps to store things. Cars go in the garage. Bikes are in the garage. _____

(A) We cook dinner in the kitchen.

(B) My sister and I rode our bikes.

(C) Outdoor toys and tools are in the garage.

15.   _____ Heat does not harm camels. They can live awhile without water. Camels eat plants.

(A) Camels live in deserts.

(B) Camels do not live in deserts.

(C) Some plants grow in deserts.

16.   One dozen is a group of twelve things. Roses can be sold by the dozen. Eggs can be sold by the dozen. _____

(A) Bagels can be sold by the dozen too.

(B) Bananas are sold by the bunch.

(C) Roses come in many colors.

17.   There once was a queen with a beautiful garden. She had silver flowers. _____ By the next day, another silver flower was in its place.

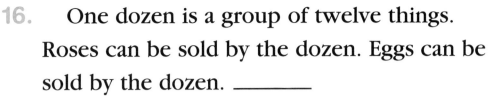

(A) The king did not like his chair.

(B) The queen sent a letter.

(C) The queen picked a silver flower each day.

18.   Many baby animals have special names. A baby kangaroo is a joey. _____ A baby cat is a kitten. A baby duck is a duckling.

(A) A father cow is a bull.

(B) A baby dog is a puppy.

(C) Some birds are born without feathers.

A. Exercising Your Skill

Number your paper from 1 to 4. Read each sentence below. Use a word from the box only once to fill in each blank correctly.

Details	closing	Complete	topic

1. ____ paragraphs have three main parts.

2. A paragraph starts with a ____ sentence.

3. ____ give information about the topic of a paragraph.

4. A ____ sentence sums up the main idea of a paragraph.

B. Expanding Your Skill

Write **A, B,** or **C** on your paper to choose the closing sentence for the end of this paragraph.

Summer will be busy. In June, my family and I are going to Montana. My grandparents live there. I go to soccer camp in July. We have many pool parties and picnics in August.

(A) I like shopping for school supplies.
(B) I like helping my mom and dad cook.
(C) I like doing fun things in the summer.

C. Exploring Language

Personal Writing Number your paper from 1 to 4. Read the paragraph below. Write the letter of the closing sentence. Then write the letter of each detail that does *not* give information about the topic.

(A) My sister and I went to the fair.
(B) We went into a barn that had horses.
(C) The barn smelled like hay. (D) The pen is on the desk. (E) Most of the horses were brown. (F) A man let us pet one of his horses. (G) Your cup is on the table. (H) Pears taste good. (I) The horse felt smooth and soft. (J) We had fun at the fair!

D. Expressing Yourself

Do one of these things. When you are done, give your paper to your teacher.

1. Draw a horse. Write a topic sentence, two details, and a closing sentence about the horse.

2. **WORK with a PARTNER** With a partner, write about horses. Write a topic sentence, three details, and a closing sentence to have a complete paragraph.

Every sentence in a paragraph should give details or tell more about the topic sentence.

Which sentence does *not* belong in each paragraph?

1. **(A)** I have a flower garden. **(B)** There are roses in my garden. **(C)** There are rocks in the front yard. **(D)** There are daisies in my garden.

2. **(A)** I like to visit the ocean. **(B)** The library closes early on Sunday. **(C)** My dad goes swimming with me. **(D)** Then my mom and dad walk with me along the shore.

3. **(A)** When it is time for lunch, we all go to the lunchroom. **(B)** Some of us bring our own lunches. **(C)** Some of us buy our lunches at school. **(D)** Gym class is after math class.

4.   **(A)** Fairy tales are make-believe stories. **(B)** There can be make-believe animals in fairy tales. **(C)** This store is full of books. **(D)** Some places in fairy tales are real though.

5.   **(A)** I ride a bus to school. **(B)** My birthday is in June. **(C)** My brother's birthday is in August. **(D)** My parents were both born in October.

6.   **(A)** Rabbits are shy animals. **(B)** They usually run away when they hear a noise. **(C)** Dogs are many sizes. **(D)** Rabbits can be afraid of other animals.

7.   **(A)** Mick took his lunch to school. **(B)** Mick plays football. **(C)** He has an apple and milk. **(D)** Mick also has a ham-and-cheese sandwich.

Which sentence does *not* belong in each paragraph?

8.   (A) My father is from Japan. (B) He speaks Japanese. (C) He can also read Japanese. (D) Chinese food tastes good.

9.   (A) Tomato plants grow best in warmer weather. (B) Tomato plants need lots of sun and water. (C) Many trees can be in cold places. (D) Tomato plants will not grow if the weather is too cold.

10.   (A) My parents have a silver car. (B) Street signs can show us what to do. (C) Street signs show us where we are going. (D) Some street signs tell us to stop.

11.   (A) Eyeglasses can help people see better. (B) I lost my key. (C) Their frames can be many colors. (D) Eyeglasses can be round or square.

12.   **(A)** Once upon a time a king lived in a forest. **(B)** The king had a daughter. **(C)** The king's daughter was a princess. **(D)** There are many trees in the park.

13.   **(A)** Snails move by gliding. **(B)** They have shells on their backs. **(C)** Some snakes have fangs. **(D)** Snails can hide inside their shells.

14.   **(A)** I drew a picture of a race car. **(B)** Rita likes to paint. **(C)** Rita painted a cloud.
(D) Rita is almost finished painting a tree.

15.   **(A)** A taco can have different foods in it.
(B) This soup has noodles. **(C)** Cheese, lettuce, and tomatoes can go in a taco.
(D) Meat and beans can go in a taco.

Which sentence does *not* belong in each paragraph?

16. **(A)** Firefighters try to save the lives of animals and people who are in danger. **(B)** Firefighters put out fires. **(C)** Firefighters have special tools and clothes to go into burning buildings. **(D)** There is a school by our house.

17. **(A)** A bank is a place where people put their money. **(B)** A post office is a place where people mail letters. **(C)** At the bank, people can borrow money. **(D)** Bank workers try to keep money safe.

18. **(A)** My dog is very playful. **(B)** He likes to chase after a ball when I throw it. **(C)** Our neighbors have a fence in their backyard. **(D)** My dog also brings his other toys for me to throw.

19.   **(A)** Simon gave his mother a poem on her birthday. **(B)** Clay can be molded into many shapes. **(C)** It can be molded into animals. **(D)** Clay can be used to make pots too.

20.   **(A)** Spiders can make webs. **(B)** Most spiderwebs are light and sticky. **(C)** A bug will probably stick to a web if the bug lands on it. **(D)** Some caterpillars feel fuzzy.

21.   **(A)** There are three children in my family. **(B)** The ruler is on the desk. **(C)** I have a brother named Jon. **(D)** I have a sister named Jess.

22.   **(A)** A tricycle has three wheels. **(B)** You ride a tricycle like you ride a bicycle. **(C)** She has a wagon. **(D)** You sit on the seat, put your feet on the pedals, and then move the pedals.

Time and order words tell when things happen. In a paragraph, they help a writer move from one detail to the next.

I shopped **today**. **Tomorrow** I will clean.

Field Trip

Read the details from a paragraph. Which time and order word completes each detail?

1. Our class will go to the library ____.

   (A) tomorrow   **(B)** yesterday

2. ____ we will read some books.

   (A) Before   **(B)** Then

3. ____ we finish reading, we will eat lunch.

   (A) After   **(B)** Next

4. The ____ thing our class will do is go home.

   (A) then   **(B)** last

Rainy Day

5. ___ was a sunny day.

   (A) Yesterday   **(B)** Next

6. ___ is a very rainy day.

   (A) Today   **(B)** Tomorrow

7. ___ we cannot go to the park.

   (A) After   **(B)** Now

8. The ___ thing we will do is wait.

   (A) next   **(B)** then

9. ___ we will hope it stops raining.

   (A) Then   **(B)** Before

10. We may go to the park ___.

    (A) yesterday   **(B)** tomorrow

Which time and order word completes the detail in each paragraph?

11. After Samuel woke up this morning, he ate breakfast. Next he brushed his teeth. Then Samuel put his lunch into his backpack. The ___ thing Samuel did was get on the bus.

(A) now   (B) last

12. At the beginning of fall, leaves can be yellow, orange, and red. ___ they turn brown. Then the leaves fall from the trees to the ground.

(A) After   (B) Next

13. To make a salad, ___ cut the vegetables. Next put the vegetables in a bowl. Then pour salad dressing on the vegetables in the bowl. Finally mix together the salad and dressing.

(A) first   (B) then

14.   Frogs need water to lay their eggs. The eggs can hatch in a few days or weeks. Frog babies are called tadpoles. They can swim. Tadpoles look like tiny fish ____ they become frogs.

(A) before   **(B)** next

15.   I had fun at camp. On Monday we rode horses. On Tuesday we hiked. On ____ we swam. On Thursday and Friday we made kites.

(A) Wednesday   **(B)** Saturday

16.   My class will have a spelling test ____. I am going to study tonight. First I will read the spelling words. Next my brother will say the words to me. Finally I will spell the words for him.

(A) yesterday   **(B)** tomorrow

A. Exercising Your Skill

Number your paper from 1 to 3. Read each sentence below. Use a word from the box only once to fill in each blank correctly.

when	detail	topic

1. Every sentence in a paragraph should tell more about the ___ sentence.

2. Time and order words tell ___ things happen.

3. Time and order words help a writer move from one ___ to the next.

B. Expanding Your Skill

Number your paper from 1 to 6. Read the paragraph below. If an underlined word is a time and order word, write *yes* on your paper. If not, write *no*.

We all helped wash the car <u>today</u>. <u>First</u> I got a pail. <u>Next</u> my brother put car soap in the pail. <u>Then</u> my dad filled the pail with water. My mom got the sponges <u>and</u> towels. <u>After</u> we dried off the car, we took it for a ride.

C. Exploring Language

Narrative Writing Number your paper from 1 to 5. Read the story below. Write the letter of each detail that does *not* stay on topic with the story.

The Talking Teddy

(A) I got a special teddy bear. (B) I named my teddy bear Baxter. (C) I have a yellow hat. (D) Baxter can talk. (E) The store is open. (F) I read the sign. (G) Baxter told me that he likes his name. (H) The dishes are dirty. (I) I told Baxter that I like his gray fur. (J) Your bike is in the garage.

D. Expressing Yourself

Do one of these things. When you are done, give your paper to your teacher.

1. Draw a teddy bear. Write a short paragraph to describe the bear. Remember to stay on topic.

2. WORK with a PARTNER Find a partner. Tell one another how to get to the other's desk. Use time and order words, such as *Then walk by the red chair.* Write the time and order words you and your partner used.

PARAGRAPHS Scope and Sequence • Specific Skill Series for Language Arts

Unit/Level	Level A	Level B	Level C	Level D	Level E	Level F	Level G	Level H
Unit 1	Types of Paragraphs	Types of Paragraphs	Types of Paragraphs	Types of Paragraphs	Narrative Paragraphs	Narrative Paragraphs	Narrative Paragraphs	Narrative Paragraphs
Unit 2	Types of Paragraphs	Using a Web	Using a Web	Using a Web	Narrative Paragraphs	Narrative Paragraphs	Narrative Paragraphs	Narrative Paragraphs
Unit 3	Using a Web	Topic Sentences	Topic Sentences	Topic Sentences	Narrative Paragraphs	Narrative Paragraphs	Narrative Paragraphs	Narrative Paragraphs
Unit 4	Topic Sentences	Details	Details	Details	Narrative Paragraphs	Narrative Paragraphs	Narrative Paragraphs	Narrative Paragraphs
Unit 5	Topic Sentences	Closing Sentences	Closing Sentences	Closing Sentences	Persuasive Paragraphs	Persuasive Paragraphs	Persuasive Paragraphs	Narrative Paragraphs
Unit 6	Details	Complete Paragraphs	Complete Paragraphs	Complete Paragraphs	Persuasive Paragraphs	Persuasive Paragraphs	Persuasive Paragraphs	Persuasive Paragraphs
Unit 7	Closing Sentences	Staying on Topic	Staying on Topic	Staying on Topic	Persuasive Paragraphs	Persuasive Paragraphs	Persuasive Paragraphs	Persuasive Paragraphs
Unit 8	Complete Paragraphs	Time and Order Words	Time and Order Words	Transition Words	Persuasive Paragraphs	Persuasive Paragraphs	Persuasive Paragraphs	Persuasive Paragraphs
Unit 9	Staying on Topic	Using Dialogue	Using Dialogue	Sentence Variety	Expository Paragraphs	Persuasive Paragraphs	Persuasive Paragraphs	Persuasive Paragraphs
Unit 10	Time and Order Words	Making Comparisons	Making Comparisons	Using Dialogue	Expository Paragraphs	Expository Paragraphs	Persuasive Paragraphs	Persuasive Paragraphs
Unit 11				Figurative Language	Writing Paragraphs	Expository Paragraphs	Expository Paragraphs	Persuasive Paragraphs
Unit 12					Writing Paragraphs	Writing Paragraphs	Expository Paragraphs	Expository Paragraphs
Unit 13					Writing Paragraphs	Writing Paragraphs	Writing Paragraphs	Expository Paragraphs
Unit 14						Writing Paragraphs	Writing Paragraphs	Writing Paragraphs
Unit 15							Writing Paragraphs	Writing Paragraphs
Unit 16								Writing Paragraphs